The Reflection Tree

The Reflection Tree

A J Bialo

Bialo Publications, Inc.
Syracuse, New York

Copyright © 2009 by Bialo Publications, Inc.
All rights reserved. Published in the United States
by Bialo Publications, Inc., Syracuse New York.

First Edition
First Printing

All of the poems featured in
The Reflection Tree are the original
Work of A J Bialo

No part of this book may be reproduced in whole or
in part without written permission of the publisher
except in reviews of critical writing. For personal
orders or other information write
Bialo Publications
PO Box 6314
Syracuse, NY 13217

ISBN: 978-0-9822232-0-8

Cover Design and Illustration by Kathryn Travalee

To Rob Flower
who gave me the gift of
putting pen to paper.

Contents

Acquisitions

Can we ever have enough?
When collecting certain stuff?
Visiting shops and little boutiques,
Looking for those special antiques.
Jewelry, furniture and artwork too,
Are just a few things you can view.
Never having inhibitions,
About making acquisitions.

Buying both used and new,
With many stacks, wading through.
Movie vidcos and DVD's,
Albums, tapes and MP3's.
Always making time to look,
At what is new amongst the books.
Sometimes buying first editions,
Selectively making acquisitions.

But sometimes you will come across,
A time when you must take a loss.
Some things simply we misplace,
Because we truly need more space.
Some things, as a matter of course,
Become split up because of divorce.
Losing things through attrition,
Starting over, making acquisitions.

Sitting in a now empty estate,
It's time to seriously redecorate.
Some items you choose to redeem,
Focusing on a certain theme.
Piece by piece, slowly collecting,
A new style you're projecting.
Always room for more additions,
We keep on making acquisitions.

Anticipation

A feeling flows upon the wind,
The voice I hear seems akin.
The past, it has so many ghosts,
Their subtle message has me engrossed.
Sometimes it feels that you are near,
I look to the horizon, for you to appear.
Although you physically do no show,
Your presence, on the wind, still blows.
Patiently I sit and wait,
Leaving things to the hand of fate.
Feeling like I cannot persuade,
From the wind your presence fades.
As another season has come and gone,
From the winds you have withdrawn.
Not knowing why you went astray,
I know you are never far away.
Until we meet I will somehow cope,
For I will never give up hope.
As the wind again blows the same affirmation,
I sit and wait, with anticipation.

Black Hole Blues

Staring out through eyes that are cold,
At a young age feeling so old.
Shutting out feelings that cause much pain,
Towards yourself you feel so much disdain.
Curling up tightly, you begin to cry,
As darkness creeps in you wish you could die.
In a place absent of colorful hues,
Beginning to sink into the black hole blues.

Blackness, which feels darker than coal,
Constantly eats away at the soul.
The black hole envelops, like a shroud,
Making it easy to feel alone in a crowd.
Feeling helpless, giving up hope,
Being sucked in, unable to cope.
Always tired and ready to snooze,
Trying to escape the black hole blues.

Within the hole there is no sound,
A deafening silence looms all around.
Watching others make idle chatter,
Seeing motion, but not hearing the clatter.
Even thoughts no longer exist,
The blackness is too much for them to resist.
Without a sound from which to take cues,
Sinking deeper, into the black hole blues.

Within the hole, there is no light,
A swirling darkness is the only sight.
Falling deeper, into a bottomless pit,
Into a darkness that seems infinite.
Spinning out of control, wishing it would stop,
Wanting to find your way back on top.
The darkness seems to tighten, like a noose,
Out of control, in the black hole blues.

Within the hole there is no peace,
The downward spiral never seems to cease.
Inwards, demons cause your soul to cry,
Outwards, cold eyes remain aridly dry.
A desperate feeling begins to swell,
Feeling you're plunging into the depths of hell.
You silently scream, I've paid my dues!
While demons drag you deeper into the black hole blues.

Within the hole, there is no time,
It seems to consume without reason or rhyme.
Noon feels like midnight, as reality slips,
Darkness shades the sun, like an eclipse.
Moving about, in a seeming trance,
Previously important things, no longer have relevance.
Day and night you can easily confuse,
The deeper you sink into the black hole blues.

Within the hole, there is no faith,
From nothing can you draw inner strength.
Knowing no longer in what to believe,
Feeling you're wearing your heart on your sleeve.
Yearning for solace, in the form of a hug,
A warm embrace that makes you feel snug.
Stuck in a dimension you did not choose,
Another day spent in the black hole blues.

The blues themselves are not a constant state,
From time to time they do abate.
They're brought on by memories of long ago,
Legacies of abuse, you do not outgrow.
It's triggered by words, or certain sounds,
Something so simple takes on the profound.
Memories of abuse, and their toxic residues,
Living on the edge of the black hole blues.

For those of you not sharing my views,
To the lucky ones, there must be a few.
To never have suffered at another one's hand,
Made to feel you can't live up to demand.
To those who have never paid the price,
To you I offer this advice.
Do not judge me, unless you've walked in my shoes,
And experienced first hand the black hole blues.

Catnap

Letting out a lengthy yawn,
Just before the break of dawn.
After a busy night of play,
Time to snooze the day away.
A quick bath, licking paws,
Taking time to trim the claws.
Finding a blanket in which to wrap,
Time to take another catnap.

A familiar sound from the kitchen does come,
As the can opener begins to hum.
Stretching the nose to glean a whiff,
Time to get up for a detailed sniff.
Leaping quickly off the bed,
Knowing it's time to be fed.
Leaving behind not a single scrap,
Time to take another catnap.

Contently sitting, licking chops,
From the window watching raindrops.
Outside, it's dark and dreary,
Inside it's warm and cheery.
Needing to feel safe and snug,
Deciding it's time to get a hug.
Seeking out a familiar lap,
Time to take another catnap.

Crawling out of a nice warm sack,
Time to grab a little snack.
Eating dry food at first,
Working up a terrible thirst.
Leaping up on the sink,
Teetering for balance on the brink.
After a quick drink from the tap,
Time to take another catnap.

Just about this time each day,
Feeling frisky, time to play.
Ignoring toys with all the fluff,
Don't like all that store bought stuff.
A piece of paper, or rubber ball,
Something to chase on down the hall.
Hiding the toy with a little paw slap,
Time to take another catnap.

Tis the life of a domestic cat,
Being lazy and getting fat.
Getting into things, requiring admonition,
Giving love, without condition.
Gently stroking thick soft fur,
Letting out a contented purr.
Forgiven any minor mishap,
Time to take another catnap.

Confusion

There are days, I often find,
I truly think I've lost my mind.
For though, I know, I've had no grog,
My mind still feels it's in a fog.
Of late it seems life is a drain,
For thoughts escape my muddled brain.
Perhaps a brain cell revolution,
Is causing me so much confusion.

And when the fog seems too thick,
Do others notice right and quick?
That their voice I cannot hear,
Even though they're standing near?
That through all the foggy steam,
Their words can't penetrate my dream.
Don't they know they're an intrusion?
Adding more to my confusion?

My mental ramblings, not always bliss,
Do other people run amiss?
Or could I be the only one,
Who feels their mind has come undone?
Not really feeling up to task,
Hiding behind illusions mask.
Is it real or just Illusion?
Or am I lost in my own confusion?

Control Freak

We all know someone in our life,
A father, mother, husband or wife.
Who feels they alone know what's best,
For me and you, and all the rest.
They stuck by you, when no one else would,
They're only looking out for your own good.
Forced to listen when they speak,
What makes one a control freak?

If you don't listen to what they say,
For your actions you will dearly pay.
They are unable to listen to reason,
Any disagreement is considered high treason.
To be successful, follow their advice,
Even if their logic is not so precise.
Giving advice that you did not seek,
What makes one a control freak?

Expected always to follow their ways,
To blindly follow till your dying days.
Forced to conform to win their love,
Forced in line, like a bad fitting glove.
Their controlling ways does effect,
The development of any self respect.
Without their help you'd be dead in a week,
What makes one a control freak?

Assigned forever to a second class,
Made to feel like you're dumb as an ass.
As they go, they make up the rules,
Making you feel like a complete fool.
For yourself you should not think,
Within yourself you begin to sink.
Always under a strict critique,
What makes one a control freak?

Your eyes have lost their familiar gleam,
As you give up hope of living your dream.
They're aware that you're under their thumb,
Normal feelings all have gone numb.
Everyday they do assail,
Existence becomes a barless jail.
Feeling your life is on a losing streak,
What makes one a control freak?

Then one day, they're no longer there,
For their absence you did not prepare.
Feeling a presence that cannot be seen,
What does their absence really mean?
With their absence you are alone,
Self-esteem has already been blown.
Another's approval you can longer seek,
What makes one a control freak?

Slowly you realize your life must go on,
Personal responsibility is a new phenomenon.
At first life goes painfully slow,
Not knowing in which direction to go.
Life is a series of trials and errors,
As you face your deepest terrors.
Life will never necessarily be chic,
What makes one a control freak?

Learning anew, life's social graces,
To appropriately act in social places.
To a new life you begin to adjust,
With other people you begin to build trust.
Slowly sharing small parts of your hell,
Little by little, coming out of your shell.
Noticing people listen when you speak,
What makes one a control freak?

Your hopes and dreams re-emerge,
As your energy begins to surge.
Their damaging influence, you try to erase,
Kinder ways you try to embrace.
Knowing you're finally on the right track,
Vowing never to allow a look back.
As a person you're no longer weak,
What makes one a control freak?

Flying High

Beaten up and beaten down,
On the edge of a nervous breakdown.
To yourself you do confess,
Recognizing your life is a mess.
Life has lost all direction,
Time to pause for some introspection.
Your body aches, your mouth is dry,
Toking up and flying high.

All your life you've done what you should,
Although your motives are misunderstood.
Letting your conscious lead the way,
Never letting yourself be led astray.
Sitting quietly with a blank stare,
Telling yourself you really don't care.
Giving up, vowing not to cry,
Toking up and flying high.

Feigning normalcy, you go to work,
Responsibility you cannot shirk.
Most of those on the job,
Take your quietness for being a snob.
The minutes slowly tick away,
Bringing to a close yet another day.
Returning home you let out a sigh,
Toking up and flying high.

Arriving home in a mood most foul,
On your face you wear a scowl.
Surrounded by a quiet solitude,
It's time to find a new attitude.
You grab your stash and fill the bowl,
Finding relief is the only goal.
The bad mood begins to slip on by,
Toking up and flying high.

As it begins to take effect,
You feel yourself disconnect.
Your mind begins to float away,
From all the stresses of the day.
Physically feeling overtaxed,
Letting go, becoming relaxed.
A peacefulness you can't deny,
Toking up and flying high.

Finally finding a content peace,
Grateful for a temporary release.
Body and mind begin to get tired,
Reflecting on the day and what transpired.
Wondering what tomorrow will bring,
Hoping it won't be too harrowing.
Closing your eyes, bidding the day goodbye,
Toking up and flying high.

Fortress Walls

Eyes, clouded like smoky glass,
No longer notice time pass.
Nor do they see the ornate gate,
Its rusted hinges and key plate.
The ivy, thick and over grown,
Hides the mortared rock and stone.
Sometimes we don't have the wherewithal,
To know we're hiding behind fortress walls.

Shouting names we don't understand,
Is often followed by a walloping backhand.
Trying, hopelessly, to please,
Knowing life could quickly cease.
Exposed to many types of assault,
Made to believe it's somehow your fault.
Brick by brick, growing tall,
Building up the fortress walls.

Always looking for a quick escape,
Life takes on a cyclical shape.
Into another's arms we quickly run,
Looking for safety, but finding none.
Repeating the past with those we date,
Over and over we relive the hate.
The numerous times, we don't want to recall,
It's safer to hide behind fortress walls.

The key, you learn to your chagrin,
Is not to let anyone in.
Refusing, again, to be led astray,
Keeping danger safe at bay.
From outside pain, feeling immune,
Wrapped up safely in a little cocoon.
Feeling safe is one of the downfalls,
Of hiding behind fortress walls.

But not everyone who shows you charm,
Is actually out to do you harm.
Actually liking what they see,
Intent is expressed quite genuinely.
There is no thought to deceive,
There are no tricks up their sleeve.
But when something good comes and calls,
Will you notice from behind fortress walls?

Turning down another advance,
Deciding not to take the chance.
Not wanting to get hurt again,
Sticking to a lonely regimen.
Life becomes run of the mill,
Knowing the hole inside we will never fill.
Progress in life continuously stalls,
Until we come out from behind fortress walls.

Freedom's Quest

The one thing universally given,
To search for freedom each person's driven.
From the moment of birth until we die,
We yearn to let our spirit fly.
But the simple concept, universally craved,
Is enjoyed by few, leaving masses depraved.
To the masses, who are socially repressed,
Join up now, on freedom's quest.

The first thing that we must achieve,
Freedom's meaning, we must conceive.
For different people have different dreams,
About what freedom really means.
It is not enough to simply say,
Freedom means I get my way.
Along the journey there is no rest,
Continuing on, in freedom's quest.

Freedom, for some, is about religion,
Which one depends on geographic region.
Praying for guidance from the divine,
Hoping to receive some sort of sign.
Following gods' divine plan,
Is the only freedom for lowly man.
But who's to say which religion is best?
Continuing on, in freedom's quest.

And then there are those who do not believe,
We ever descended from Adam and Eve.
Developing from a biological chain,
Because we adapted we still remain.
We all must have a strong inner drive,
Knowing that only the strong survive.
Often this theory leaves many distressed,
Continuing on, in freedom's quest.

No matter what your personal belief,
From oppression we all seek relief.
While these two views are the extremes,
We must find the middle to realize the dream.
Putting aside where we began,
No one is better or lesser than.
In one and all we must invest,
Continuing on, in freedom's quest.

Assume for a moment there is no god,
No omnipotent to give us a prod.
Suppose all there is, is good mother earth,
Suppose we determine our own self worth.
Self contained on our own little globe,
What relevance now has the trials of Job?
These are all issues not often addressed,
Continuing on, in freedom's quest.

Not often addressed because we're afraid,
To think our existence is wholly man made.
In the absence of a universal plan,
Everyone is equal, both woman and man.
Without supreme guidance from above,
We must learn the art of self-love.
We are no different than all the rest,
Continuing on, in freedom's quest.

Breaking down barriers that kept us apart,
Leveling the playing field with a new start.
Whether black or white, or in between,
All have the right to be heard and seen.
Throwing aside class or caste,
All must put behind the uneven past.
What is now allowed was once repressed,
Continuing on, in freedom's quest.

The first thing we must admit,
All types of behavior we must permit.
Revising our code or moral law,
There can be no sin or character flaw.
There can be no room for prejudice,
Together we must learn to co-exist.
With a new morality we now must wrest,
Continuing on, in freedom's quest.

Who's to say what's right or wrong?
Is survival really for the strong?
What of those who are physically weak?
Or those who simply just are meek?
How do we ensure equality,
To satisfy more than the majority.
Not something we can take in jest,
Continuing on, in freedom's quest.

Must freedom always have a limit?
Are there certain things we can't permit?
In deciding where to draw the line,
Certain freedoms we must resign.
On others rights we can't infringe,
Or society itself we will unhinge.
Avoiding great civil unrest,
Continuing on, in freedom's quest.

Lacking a well thought out plan,
Wondering if it's too utopian.
To heal the chasm which divides,
Requires many ground breaking strides.
Keeping the goal always in sight,
Together we must continue to fight.
All we can do is do our best,
Continuing on, in freedom's quest.

The Long Goodbye

Beginning to get up there in age,
When you start to notice a change.
It starts out happening once in a while,
Conversations take on a cyclical style.
The same questions and comments, again and again,
You are not the same person that I knew when.
Going round and round I sit and sigh,
And so we start the long goodbye.

A mind, that once was sharp as a tack,
Slowly and surely begins to slack.
Like a shadow that has been cast,
Living further and further in the past.
Agitated, you want to roam,
Not realizing you're already home.
Within my silencc I sit and cry,
As we continue with the long goodbye.

Just sitting and staring,
Through blank eyes, uncaring.
Lost in a very distant place,
Unable to recognize a familiar face.
Trying hard to converse,
While your mind runs in reverse.
Unable to even try,
As we continue with the long goodbye.

No longer knowing the time of day,
As the mind continues to slip away.
No longer willing to eat,
Meal time is a daunting feat.
No longer aware of hygiene,
Wearing the same clothes, unclean.
Body follows mind, on a downward slide,
As we continue the long goodbye.

And so it goes, year after year,
Muddled thoughts, paranoia and fear.
Each new day brings ups and downs,
Becoming weaker, less smiles, more frowns.
Finally giving up the fight,
You fade into that dark good night.
As your soul moves towards the sky,
Finally we must say our last goodbye.

Masks

From many I've heard say,
Life is just a game to play.
During the game we all know,
Your whole hand you never show.
That which we choose to hide,
We keep closely by our side.
Depending on the current task,
We all put on a certain mask.

But does the game ever end?
Do the rules ever bend?
Are there those that we let in?
With whom we can be genuine?
Or has the mask become a regime,
Forcing others to the outer extreme?
For in what pleasure could we bask,
If we always wear a mask?

For some because a mask is new,
Opaqueness lets you see right through.
For those who have learned the trick,
After much betrayal it becomes quite thick.
Whether they're color, or black and white,
Their mystery always seems to invite.
But would one ever dare to ask,
Are you for real? Or just a mask?

Melancholy Home

The whistle blows, another crossing past,
Rolling ever closer, to destination last.
Rolling ever closer, rocking back and forth,
Waiting for arrival at 7th and 34th.
Stepping on the platform, people rushing by,
Family and loved ones embrace, some even cry.
Once upon the city streets, my feet begin to roam,
Without thought of direction, in my melancholy home.

The streets look all the same to me, dirty and worn,
Congested city streets, with cabbies honking horns.
I sit and watch the people, quickly walking by,
Eyes transfixed on pavement, never noticing the sky.
A random chance at eye contact, I quickly give a nod,
Contact quickly broken, his expression says you're odd.
I look beyond the people, into my private gloam,
Retreating ever deeper, in my melancholy home.

I take the subway downtown, on board the number nine,
Consumed with my thoughts, I reach the end of the line.
Large crowds are milling, throughout Battery Park,
Waiting for the ferry and their chance to embark.
To visit lady liberty which the French did bequeath,
And read her words of inspiration, inscribed beneath.
I set my sights farther, beyond the metal and chrome,
Across the bay I long to be, in my melancholy home.

The bridges vast expanse, lay before my eyes.
For a chance to touch the past, my soul inwardly cries.
Within the city limits, laying beneath the earth,
Is the missing puzzle piece, which consummated birth.
Facts revealing identity, have all fallen through,
Secrets and lies compounded, give not the slightest clue.
Guessing at the truth, perhaps an incestual chromosome,
I just can't help but wonder, in my melancholy home.

Allowing one last look back, I turn and walk away.
Never getting closer, feeling empty and dismayed.
While riding on the subway, uptown on the one,
I sat pondering intently, what more I could have done.
Without an answer pending, I went looking for a pint,
Ending up in a little pub near 8th and 59th.
The bartender pours a draft, I sip it through the foam.
And vow to solve the mystery of my melancholy home.

The whistle blows, it is now time to depart,
As the train begins to move, I feel sadness in my heart.
Deeds left undone, words never said,
Endless possibilities running through my head.
Rolling ever farther, the train is changing track.
As the skyline begins to fade, I allow one last look back.
The puzzle incomplete, still unable to go home,
I must content myself, for now, in my melancholy home.

Missing You

As we journey down our road,
We each carry our own load.
But when the load's too hard to bear,
We seek out someone with which to share.
Sharing the secrets of the soul,
Each others sadness we would console.
A friend met, out of the blue,
Today I sit here missing you.

Never feeling the need to please,
Together we are well at ease.
For words we need never sought,
Knowing what the other thought.
Trusting in the hands of fate,
I feel you are my kindred mate.
From the start I somehow knew,
I'd sit here missing you.

As each month would fly on by,
We'd let out another sigh.
For many things we'd yet to do,
Side by side, just me and you.
One by one we'd knock them off,
Never once did I hear you scoff.
Recalling projects we got through,
As I sit here, missing you.

In simple ways we did have fun,
Chatting in the summer sun.
Often we would spend our time,
Engaging in a game of rhyme.
While working on linguistic form,
We'd revel in a passing storm.
Taking in each day anew,
Today I sit here, missing you.

And as your health began to fade,
Never once were you afraid.
Already having made your peace,
Welcoming your final release.
As you laid there in your bed,
Dreams were running through your head.
Privately doing a life review,
I sat by your side, missing you.

Our time together, although brief,
Still leaves me feeling intense grief.
Sitting quietly, I say your name,
Knowing I'll never be the same.
Our journey, having met its end,
My heart, someday, will surely mend.
Although I've bid you fond adieu,
I still sit here, missing you.

Nobody's Child

A child is born that cannot be kept,
The mother, exhausted, silently wept.
But not too exhausted to feel the rage,
Of being forced, into a cage.
Family members leave you no choice,
Leaving you without a voice.
Feeling as if you've been defiled,
Beginning to feel like nobody's child.

The minute the baby is out of the womb,
A nurse ushers it out of the room.
The mother is never allowed to see,
Her own child after delivery.
After all she might change her mind,
Become attached, become intertwined.
Making sure all papers are filed,
After giving birth to nobody's child.

The process begins to find a new home,
As the baby lies in a crib made of chrome.
Every year many couples apply,
Unfortunately many they must deny.
Those who qualify are put on a list,
After years of waiting they still persist.
A short list is quickly compiled,
To find a home for nobody's child.

Many times they tried on their own,
Never succeeding for reasons unknown.
Giving up, they finally opt,
Deciding it's best if they adopt.
Beginning their family they need not postpone,
Good news finally comes on the phone.
The perspective parents eagerly smiled,
Taking custody of nobody's child.

The baby delivered right to their door,
The first year the agency will monitor.
Visited each week by a social worker,
Making sure you're not a shirker.
During that year never giving up hope,
Examining their lives under a microscope.
After a year they've passed their trial,
Giving them the rights to nobody's child.

Finally the child they can call their own,
Excitedly calling relatives, on the phone.
The first thing they do is give a new name,
Saving the babe from certain shame.
Changing records that act as a shield,
Records that remain permanently sealed.
After their trial final papers are filed,
Legally adopting nobody's child.

But the real trial is about to begin,
Figuring out how to fit in.
Not all family members are overjoyed,
In fact, some are outright annoyed.
Including someone from outside,
Some comments are downright snide.
How easily the family seems to be riled,
At the thought of including nobody's child.

Even though you are very young,
Already feeling quite high strung.
The one thing on which you've obsessed,
Is you don't look like all the rest.
Lying awake all night long,
Pondering the idea you don't belong.
Many thoughts remain unreconciled,
Pondering the thought of being nobody's child.

And then it finally happens one day,
Your parents sit you down to say.
You are so special, for it was you we picked,
For it was not in your mother that you grew and kicked.
Confronting the truth, the process begun,
Explaining you're not like other daughters or sons.
Realizing you're not really their child,
Beginning to feel like nobody's child.

Left alone to ponder what all this means,
Slipping into emptiness as deep as a ravine.
The question arises, what did I do wrong?
To be taken away from where I belong?
Circumstances remain unknown,
Your whole identity has been blown.
Keeping secrets all the while,
Telling no one you're nobody's child.

Knowing there's no place you really belong,
A feeling that remains all life long.
Feeling alone even in a crowd,
Being followed around by a big black cloud.
Trying to escape all the emotional pain,
Looking for ways to alter your brain.
As a teenager, acting very wild,
Rebelling for being nobody's child.

Figuring out who you are,
Trying to heal the emotional scar.
For the truth you must search,
Personally doing your own research.
Piecing together all of the clues,
Finally finding some really good news.
Letting emotions finally get riled,
No longer feeling like nobody's child.

Finally finding and ready to meet,
Hoping to somehow feel complete.
Finally the past begins to unroll,
Finding answers is good for the soul.
But too much time has already elapsed,
Hopes of belonging already collapsed.
Leaving some feelings still unreconciled,
Feeling, again, like nobody's child.

Slowly the realization finally sets in,
Within neither family do you truly fit in.
Now that you've physically and emotionally grown,
Family is something you must make on your own.
The only ones that you will let in,
Are those who stand by you through thick and thin.
Becoming someone completely self styled,
Realizing you are nobody's child.

Odd Marble Out

Each person is a member of a clan,
That's the way it's been, since time began.
From all over the earth clans emerged,
Into their culture, one becomes submerged.
To each clan is assigned a name,
Something each member proudly proclaims.
To a family name you she be devout,
Unless you are the odd marble out.

Membership in the clan happens at birth,
Blood lines determine one's self worth.
For those taken in, absent of blood ties,
Their existence, the clan must legitimize.
Given a lineage to call their own,
Their limited acceptance they cannot bemoan.
Knowing their membership is somehow in doubt,
It's tough to be the odd marble out.

During childhood years you get the sense,
Your existence is shrouded with false pretense.
The first thing you notice is how things appear,
The striking differences are quite clear.
The second thing noticed is how people act,
With you, there is a difference in how they interact.
So many differences noticed throughout,
To let you know you are the odd marble out.

Questions arise, in your own mind,
Why you are not with your own kind.
What could have happened? To go so wrong?
To be taken away from where you belong.
When did the secrets and lies begin?
Wondering why you just can't fit in.
With no answer forthcoming you want to shout,
Why must I be the odd marble out?

Later in life you search for the truth,
To uncover what happened in your youth.
Searching for clues, like a needle in a haystack,
Trying desperately to find your way back.
Trying to fill an ominous hole,
Which no other could ever console.
Hoping that everything will eventually turn out,
Trying to lose the feeling of odd marble out.

At first reunion you feel your soul alight,
You begin to feel that everything's alright.
As the newness wears off, problems do stem,
You begin to realize you're not really like them.
The ties that bind have never been built,
Your hopes of belonging begin to wilt.
Not prepared for all the unexpected fallout,
Realizing you're still the odd marble out.

Playing the Game

From the minute I was born,
My path in life was slowly worn.
Walking on, with each new day,
Taking on what comes my way.
I cannot change what's in the past,
Forging on, I go steadfast.
Unknowingly, into this world I came,
Destined naturally, to play the game.

I have heard from many fools,
Who are sure they know the rules.
In your life they'll interfere,
Though their motives are sincere.
Prodding you to go along,
Follow them and you'll be strong.
My free spirit they try to tame,
But I will not play their game.

With each person that I connect,
I must show some due respect.
Their many viewpoints I will hear,
Although I may not hold them dear.
For each of us must make a choice,
How best to express our voice.
Upon no one can I assign blame,
For my choices, while playing the game.

For a bit of cash I've often wished,
But still I remain impoverished.
Through the years of my life's span,
Riches do not seem part of the plan.
My friends and family are my wealth,
They boost my soul and keep my health.
I do not seek fortune and fame,
I only wish to play the game.

From time to time I feel annoyed,
With certain folks I'd rather avoid.
Those who act quite obnoxious,
Leaving me feeling very noxious.
To them, I say, just go away,
But they always return another day.
Their rude behavior I think a shame,
I do not enjoy playing their game.

The rules of life are not always fair,
But I must not give in to despair.
For what is both wonderful and strange,
Is that there are rules I can change.
This should cause no one alarm,
As long as I cause no one else harm.
The rules never remain the same,
The longer you keep playing the game.

Down the road I continue to plod,
I don't care if you think me odd.
For I will live as I see fit,
To no one else will I submit.
Within myself I am content,
Which in itself is an accomplishment.
Until death extinguishes my flame,
I will continue to play the game.

Poverty Prone

Growing up, life seems so sunny,
With no concept for the value of money
With your parents you have resided,
For you, everything has been provided.
At this time, life seems ideal,
Never worrying about your next meal.
Not knowing the world into which you'll be thrown,
Not knowing life's struggle, when you're poverty prone.

Finding a job at just seventeen,
For minimum wage, serving fast food cuisine.
Breaking your back for a few extra bucks,
Realizing quickly, this job really sucks.
Sticking it out, but counting the days,
Until graduation, and a real job that pays.
Taking care of yourself, now that you're grown,
Vowing you'll never be poverty prone.

Finally receiving a high school diploma,
Celebrations leave you close to a coma.
After a few days you sober up,
A few job interviews you need to set up.
A few job leads you do acquire,
But without experience they will not hire.
Wanting to be out, on your own,
Not wanting to start out poverty prone.

Many tell you, to become an employee,
You need at least a four-year degree.
Packing your bags, you're off to school,
To learn the industrial golden rule.
Diligently working, class after class,
Grade point credits, you do amass.
Paying for college with a student loan,
Not thinking you could become poverty prone.

After four long years you get your degree,
Celebrating your accomplishment with much glee.
The loans that you borrowed are now coming due,
Seven years of payments before you are through.
Taking the first job that comes along,
Unemployment you don't want to prolong.
Professional skills you try to hone,
Trying to avoid being poverty prone.

Now that you finally have a job,
Credit card companies are no longer snobs.
Getting credit doesn't seem very hard,
Everyone wants you to carry their card.
All you need do is just apply,
Your employment they will verify
Buying what you want, you need not postpone,
Not thinking about being poverty prone.

With the money you earn you're just getting by,
Demand for payment exceeds your supply.
You pay what you can but come up short,
Through mounds of bills you continue to sort.
Your next check won't come for a week,
Your financial picture seems quite bleak.
Seeing which bills you can postpone,
Telling yourself you're not poverty prone.

Finding a job with better pay,
Hoping to end your fiscal dismay.
New employers you try to impress,
While searching for the secret of success.
Toiling on, hour after hour,
Earning extra wages, which taxes devour.
Keeping your nose to the grindstone,
Hoping to end being poverty prone.

No further ahead than when you began,
You feel you are dancing as fast as you can.
At an insane pace you feel driven,
Not an inch of slack have you been given.
On your bills you try to catch up,
But creditors phone calls never let up.
With no forward progress you let out a groan,
Facing up to the fact you are poverty prone.

One day you wake up to discover,
From this debt you will never recover.
Creditors continue to give you grief,
From their harassment you need some relief.
For relief you finally file,
A list of creditors you must compile.
The fact that you're bankrupt you cannot bemoan,
With a chance to escape being poverty prone.

A second chance you've been given,
All your debts have been forgiven.
Learning to budget and pay in cash,
Still no reserve are you able to stash.
If you only knew then what you know now,
Maybe you life would be different somehow.
In hindsight the lesson is clearly shown,
That anyone can easily become poverty prone.

Procrastinate

For some folks it is a crime,
To even think of wasting time.
Their calendar is tightly run,
There are many things that must be done.
Every minute they must plan,
Cramming in as much as they can.
They'd never think of being late,
And never could they procrastinate.

But I, on the other hand,
Could not care to beat the band.
Daily life is much more lax,
Mind and body I will not tax.
Every moment I will enjoy,
Delay tactics I will employ.
Results I will leave up to fate,
I cannot help but procrastinate.

For those who need a strict regime,
Please don't traipse upon my daydream.
While you run, within your rush,
Do not disturb my gentle hush.
For we will never see eye to eye,
To your ways I won't comply.
Once again, I'll reiterate,
I cannot help but procrastinate.

Quilting Blues

The Names Project Memorial Quilt,
For a specific purpose has been built.
To remember the name of the brave,
Who because of AIDS went to an early grave.
Cut down in the prime of life,
At the end there's no drum and fife.
A very dear friend you did lose,
Death precedes the quilting blues.

Making a quilt requires few tools,
But before you start, you must know the rules.
The quilt must measure three by six,
Upon its surface, mementos you affix.
The hem must measure two inches around,
For to other panels it will be bound.
Follow these rules and success ensues,
Death precedes the quilting blues.

Sitting and staring at a blank cloth frame,
The first thing you lay out is their name.
Often their birth and death date,
Is something you want to incorporate.
In their honor you pick a theme,
Pictorially representing their life's dream.
Symbolically sharing the life they did choose,
Death precedes the quilting blues.

When your panel is finally done,
It's time to finish what you've begun.
Making ready for the day,
When the full quilt will be on display.
You've already made your traveling plan,
While keeping the panel as safe as you can.
Packing clothes and some comfortable shoes,
Death precedes the quilting blues.

Immediately struck by the quilts enormity,
Even checkerboard rows show its conformity.
It continues on, row after row,
Year by year it continues to grow.
Colorful panels, stretch out like a sea,
A silent reminder of a social catastrophe.
Noticing all the colorful hues,
Death precedes the quilting blues.

Giving it up is harder than you thought,
Heart strings being very distraught.
For a second time you have to let go,
Hoping your feelings don't readily show.
Assigned a number and put in a stack,
As tears flow you dare not look back.
Hoping it's included when the quilt debuts,
Death precedes the quilting blues.

Early in the morning, the next day,
Section by section they ceremoniously lay.
Eagerly awaiting it to be shown,
To see if your panel has already been sewn.
Much more time would you like to spend,
But the display has reached a timely end.
The time has come to bid last adieus,
Death precedes the quilting blues.

The Realty Game

Did I hear you say, pray tell,
You're in the market to buy or sell?
Step right up and tell me your name,
You're the next contestant in the realty game.
Sit right down, tell me what you're looking for,
A ranch perhaps, or maybe a Tudor?
Or perhaps you prefer an older Victorian,
With a detached garage to store your Delorian.
Let me know what price you can swing,
We'll have you moved in the first day of spring.
Here's a list of houses in your P.V.R.M.,
This one in specific could be a real gem.
Here's one I really think you should see,
Hold on a sec, where's my lock box key?
This house here you'll find very unique,
After a little rehab, it should look very chic.
The owner is willing to accept your offer,
Eager to move out and become a golfer.
A small down payment is all we require,
Have all the paperwork checked by your esquire.
The mortgage company is talking to banks,
For your business I want to say thanks.
The rest of the deal is handled with ease,
Could we have the next contestant please?

The Reflection Tree

Roots spreading, tree growing,
Within the wind leaves blowing.
Troubled heart, troubled mind,
Needing to escape the same old grind.
Wandering through nature, which seems so pristine,
Searching for a spot where you won't be seen.
Coming together near the banks of the sea,
Seeking refuge under the reflection tree.

Leaning against its sturdy bark,
Seeing only your own footmarks.
No one has been here, of this you are sure,
Adding to its already mystic allure.
Contentedly watching a flock of geese,
By communing with nature you find inner peace.
Crouching down letting thoughts run free,
Seeking refuge under the reflection tree.

To this place you are often drawn,
Enjoying the spectacular views at dawn.
As often as possible you slip away,
Wishing forever right here you could stay.
Its natural beauty you often crave,
As you watch sunbeams dance on the wave.
From the harshness of life you temporarily flee,
Seeking refuge under the reflection tree.

Under the tree you have often sat,
Especially after a spousal spat.
Your thoughts you slowly begin to collect,
Allowing an opportunity to introspect.
Within yourself you can be sincere,
Allowing the situation to seem more clear.
Finding a new sense of stability,
Seeking refuge under the reflection tree.

Time after time you have returned,
In solitude, many lessons you've learned.
Both you and the tree cannot be deterred,
As over time you have both matured.
Knowing your growth is not based on a whim,
Growing and learning like a tree sprouts a limb.
Growing in a place which provides security,
Seeking refuge under the reflection tree.

With no one else do you share this place,
Its natural beauty you don't want to deface.
No matter the seasonal time of year,
Its peacefulness you always revere.
This space you treat with a certain respect,
Knowing it provides a safe place to reflect.
Its continued safety you oversee,
Seeking refuge under the reflection tree.

Secrets and Lies

To move forward, you must know where you've been,
A phrase that haunts, again and again.
The truth of the matter you want to find out,
To know what your roots are really about.
For what most folks take for granted,
In your life has all been slanted.
No one could ever realize,
The damage done from secrets and lies.

You never know what to believe,
When someone you trust always deceives.
Perhaps without malicious intent,
You still must deal with abandonment.
Never able to fill the hole,
Never able to heal the soul.
The absent one, easy to despise,
All built upon secrets and lies.

Often you find your mind will wander,
The basic things you sit and ponder.
Simple questions you can't answer,
Such as in your family is there cancer?
Your hair is red, theirs is brown,
Even your voices don't make the same sound.
Just once, to look in their eyes,
To finally end the secrets and lies.

Finding a piece of the puzzle, you rejoice,
But there are still pieces missing that know no voice.
Countless hours of research you spend,
But all clues lead to dead ends.
Those who know wouldn't tell you if they could,
Told that it is all for your own good.
God forbid you criticize,
Those who perpetuate the secrets and lies.

Unwilling to give up the fight,
You continue on, knowing you're right.
Retracing old files for clues,
Disappointment causes the blues.
Sadness only one can console,
The one swallowed by the black hole.
After many years feeling demoralized,
From the perpetuation of secrets and lies.

No more of the puzzle can you unwind,
Knowing the missing you will never find.
As years keep passing, trails go cold,
While those who know still withhold.
Never losing that feeling of yearning,
A sense of resentment, deep down is burning.
Until your final breath you will despise,
The unnecessary deception, of secrets and lies.

Stirrings

Sensitive to the world around,
From simple pleasures to the profound.
Connected strongly to the universe,
At first, me thinks, it is a curse.
To see what others cannot see,
They think of me quite morbidly.
The silenced bones you are interring,
Their silent voices, still gently stirring.

They guide the voices in my mind,
Our lives, they still are intertwined.
Their essence never truly gone,
Seen in shadows between dusk and dawn.
And although we can no longer touch,
Their influence has meant so much.
With them often I'll be conferring,
Contently listening to their gentle stirring.

Their presence within the mists of time,
Help with hurdles I must climb.
In amongst the tallest trees,
Their voice, heard within the breeze.
And in the darkest depths of night,
Basking in the eternal light.
The lines of duality always blurring,
I continue to listen to their gentle stirrings.

Thoughts

I thought I'd sit and write today,
That maybe I'd have something to say.
I thought I knew what words to use,
I had not thought myself obtuse.
I thought I knew when feeling depressed,
That by writing I could express.
I thought the mangled mess inside,
I could somehow put aside.
I thought that I could use my mind,
Knowing how it worked and intertwined.
I thought that I could protect my heart,
But find I'm missing a big part.
I thought at least I had my soul,
But even that I can't console.
I thought that if I sat and cried,
I wouldn't feel as if I'd died.
I thought I knew which way to move,
That I'd finally found the groove.
I thought I knew the direction I sought,
I thought …

Twilights Last Gleam

As a feeling of sleepiness fills your head,
It's time to drag your body to bed.
As soon as your head hits the pillow,
You begin to feel very mellow.
You feel yourself drift off to sleep,
Into a darkness infinitely deep.
Then like magic you begin to dream,
Passing through the twilights last gleam.

As you pass through the dream stage,
From your body you disengage.
Your heart rate begins to slow,
As breathing becomes more shallow.
Respiration continually drops,
Until your heart suddenly stops.
Your body has lost all of its steam,
Passing through the twilights last gleam.

The weight of your body you no longer tote,
Above your body you feel yourself float.
To orient yourself you look all around,
Seeing your body as you look down.
Surprisingly enough you feel no fear,
Wondering where you'll go from here.
Floating through the darkness you see a faint beam,
Passing through the twilights last gleam.

Towards the light you feel drawn,
As entrancing as headlights are to a fawn.
Within its path you feel you are thrust,
Following along is an act of blind trust.
All control you gladly concede,
Moving along at godspeed.
Flowing along the bright white stream,
Passing through the twilights last gleam.

Whiteness more brilliant than a snow-white dove,
Surrounds you with feelings of purest love.
Your total being feels complete,
At no other time experiencing anything so sweet.
Total completeness mortals can't comprehend,
Feeling yourself continuing to ascend.
Continuing on to meet a being supreme,
Passing through the twilights last gleam.

But just as you're ready to meet the divine,
You're suddenly prevented from crossing the line.
You're met by a person that perhaps you know,
Enveloped in the bright lights glow.
They're there to tell you it's not yet your time,
That you've still much to do while still in your prime.
Permitted only to the outer extreme,
Passing through the twilights last gleam.

At first your leaving you try to resist,
For in no other place would you want to exist.
But your guide is still acting as a blockade,
Leaving you feeling very dismayed.
Beginning the long journey back,
Falling into your body with a healthy smack.
Returning back to your earthly regime,
Passing through the twilights last gleam.

Once back in your body you re-awake,
Sitting up with a bolt your body does shake.
You feel your heart pounding, deep in your chest,
What has just happened you try to digest.
Your heart starts returning to its normal beat,
Remembering your experience is bittersweet.
Realizing that nothing is as it seems,
Passing through the twilights last gleam.

Knowing forever your life has changed,
Priorities in life become rearranged.
From the material world you begin to retreat,
Paying more attention to the people you meet.
Facing the future without any fear,
Knowing you have the strength to persevere.
Realizing you're part of a grander scheme,
Passing through the twilights last gleam.

Witch's Dance

Long ago, through time and space,
I looked upon your shining face.
Eye to eye all the while,
We shared a warm inviting smile.
But just as our souls celebrate,
We played into the hands of fate.
Torn apart by circumstance,
Remember now the witch's dance.

Until the day when we could meet,
Always feeling incomplete.
Hung out on a lurch,
Never giving up the search.
Many life times would be spent,
Within this lonely lament.
Hearing the drums distant resonance,
Beckoning back to the witch's dance.

And now within this time and place,
I look again upon your shining face.
In your eyes I see a shine,
For I am yours and you are mine.
Looking deep into your soul,
My heart again is truly whole.
Now is finally our second chance,
To enjoy again the witch's dance.

Acknowledgments

On Line Journals

Poetry Magazine: *Catnap*

Little Brown Poetry: *Melancholy Home*